HORSEBACK RIDING BASICS

HORSEBACK RIDING BASICS

Written by
Dianne Reimer
with
Carol Lee

Introduction by
Gordon Wright

Illustrated by
Bill Gow

Photographs by
Vick Owens

Edited and Produced by
Arvid Knudsen

PRENTICE-HALL, INC.
Englewood Cliffs, New Jersey

Dedication

I dedicate this book to my son, Billy Reimer, who had so much generosity and love in his spirit. He gave to the world of horses.

Acknowledgment

Our very special thanks to the young people who appear in the photographs of this book: Todd Angkatavanich, Shawnee Brown, Devon Reimer and Karen Strutin and their horses.

BOOK DESIGN BY ARVID KNUDSEN

Printed in the United States of America J

Prentice-Hall International, Inc., London
Prentice-Hall of Australia, Pty. Ltd., North Sydney
Prentice-Hall of Canada, Ltd., Toronto
Prentice-Hall of India Private Ltd., New Delhi
Prentice-Hall of Japan, Inc., Tokyo
Prentice-Hall of Southeast Asia Pte. Ltd., Singapore
Whitehall Books Limited, Wellington, New Zealand

10 9 8 7 6 5 4 3 2 1

Library of Congress Cataloging in Publication Data

Reimer, Dianne.
Horseback riding basics.

Includes index.
SUMMARY: Illustrated text introduces the fundamentals of horseback riding, including the necessary equipment and locations of establishments offering riding instructions.
1. Horsemanship—Juvenile literature. [Horsemanship] I. Title.
SF309.2.R43
1980 797.2'3 80-18530
ISBN 0-13-394858-7

CONTENTS

INTRODUCTION

We have come a long way in all the things we do today. Records are being broken in every field. Training techniques have improved immensely. The quality of our athletes continues to be better. And in the field of horses, our riders are better and our horses are better. This is progress. But progress comes with commitment.

I have known Dianne Reimer for many years. She is a dedicated person with one goal; that is to be an excellent teacher and trainer.

This book has a terrific amount of good advice and it displays an immense knowledge of the field. It is very easy to read for all grades of riders.

I recommend this book for all equestrians.

Gordon Wright
Teacher, trainer and horseman

1 THE LURE AND THE LORE OF THE HORSE

Do you want to ride? Of course it would be great, and easy, if you owned a horse or pony. Not many of you can do it today, but there is a way you can ride a horse every now and then. In the following pages, you will find out how and where you can find a horse just waiting for you to ride. You will also find out how to ride.

The horse you ride may not belong to you, but for a little while you can pretend that he really is yours. You can give him a special name, he will never tell anyone, and you will always remember him as your first horse.

A Little Horse History

It was millions of years ago, and long before the coming of man, when huge and strange-looking creatures roamed and ruled the earth. The ancestry and history of the horse have been traced with the fossils (remains) of these ancient beasts.

The forefather of the modern-day horse was the *Eohippus* (pronounced E-o-hipp-us) or Dawn Horse. The Eohippus was a small animal about sixteen-inches high, the size of a collie dog. In many ways it resembled a fox. It had a long head, large eyes, and a coat spotted like a reindeer's. It had a short neck. Its mane and short tail consisted of a few stiff hairs. It had five toes on each of its front feet and three toes on each hind ones. It was not a very strong animal, but it made up for that with its speed. In this way it was able to outrun its slow-moving enemies and survive.

Centuries passed. The condition of the earth changed. With each change the Eohippus changed, too, and adapted to its environment. Each generation was a little larger and stronger than its parents had been. Its short neck and legs became longer, larger and heavier. Its mane and tail became longer and fuller. All the toes except the middle one on each foot disappeared. This remaining toe developed into a single, strong nail, which became the horse's hoof. Instead of running around on the balls of its feet like a rabbit, it now ran on its tiptoes. Its small teeth, which formerly were only sharp enough to nibble the soft wet grass of the marshlands, grew larger and developed flat surfaces. Now it was able to cut, grind, and chew the dry, coarse vegetation of the open plains. And, strangely enough, it developed an open space between its canine, or front, teeth and its back teeth. Later in history, man domesticated the horse and placed an iron bar, called a "bit", across the horse's mouth in these open spaces. And, by attaching ropes to the sides of the bit, he was able to guide and control the horse.

The little wild creature that was once only as large as a fox developed into one of the most beautiful and graceful animals on earth.

2 | RIDE FOR FUN AND FITNESS

More people, of all ages, are riding horses than ever before. The number is increasing every day. There are more horses in existence today than ever before, and more people are eager to learn about them and how to ride them. Horseback riding is fun, whether you ride in a group or by yourself. But knowing how to ride has many more advantages to it than just the enjoyment of a great sport.

A tremendous strength of character is developed in children as they acquire riding skills. At first, a child riding a horse may be anxious. But with time and training anxiety is turned into knowledge and then into pleasure. Acquiring the basic skills of horseback riding will improve a youngster's ability in other sports. It improves schoolwork, also.

Horseback riding improves overall muscle tone and coordination. All body muscles are brought into play: Leg muscles are tightened and toned; back and stomach muscles are limbered and made more pliable. Eye and hand coordination are developed to a marked degree. A sense of balance is improved. Confidence is built. And a greater appreciation and love of nature are developed.

Start Right and You Won't Go Wrong

The age at which you start horseback riding is not important. The belief that you must start at a very early age to become a fine rider is wrong. What is most important is *how* you learn.

Anyone who can catch a ball or skip a rope can learn to ride a horse. Learning to ride is not simply a matter of climbing aboard a horse and saying, "Giddee-yap, let's go." You may manage to stay mounted if it is a quiet horse and moves slowly, but this is not really riding. You, the rider, will not be able to get your horse to do what you want if you are not able to convey your wishes and instructions to your horse.

TAKE LESSONS FROM A QUALIFIED, PROFESSIONAL INSTRUCTOR.

In the beginning, you must take lessons from a qualified, professional instructor. Once you have gained knowledge of the basics, experience, and confidence, you may ride alone. This does not always come easily. Merely reading this book will not make you into a good rider. This book introduces you to the basic requirements and understanding you must have in order to apply yourself as a student of riding. Read and follow the text. With a good instructor, lots of study, and repeated practice, an appreciation and understanding of the art and sport of horsemanship will develop as you ride.

A rider must develop a sense of self-discipline while working toward the goal of being a good rider. By following the step-by-step approach to good horsemanship, it will become apparent that there is a right way and a wrong way to do everything. You must develop a sense of what is correct if you want to hasten your success.

In this book we focus only on basics. Beginners cannot absorb more. You will be introduced to the horse and its parts, tack and the proper wearing attire, where to ride, mounting—correct position, dismounting, discipline and control, the natural gaits of the horse, and other vital information. These are the minimum essentials all novices must learn and master. And so, let's go. We start with the horse.

THE HORSE

Study the picture. Learn the words that describe the different parts so that you will know them when you come across them in the text.

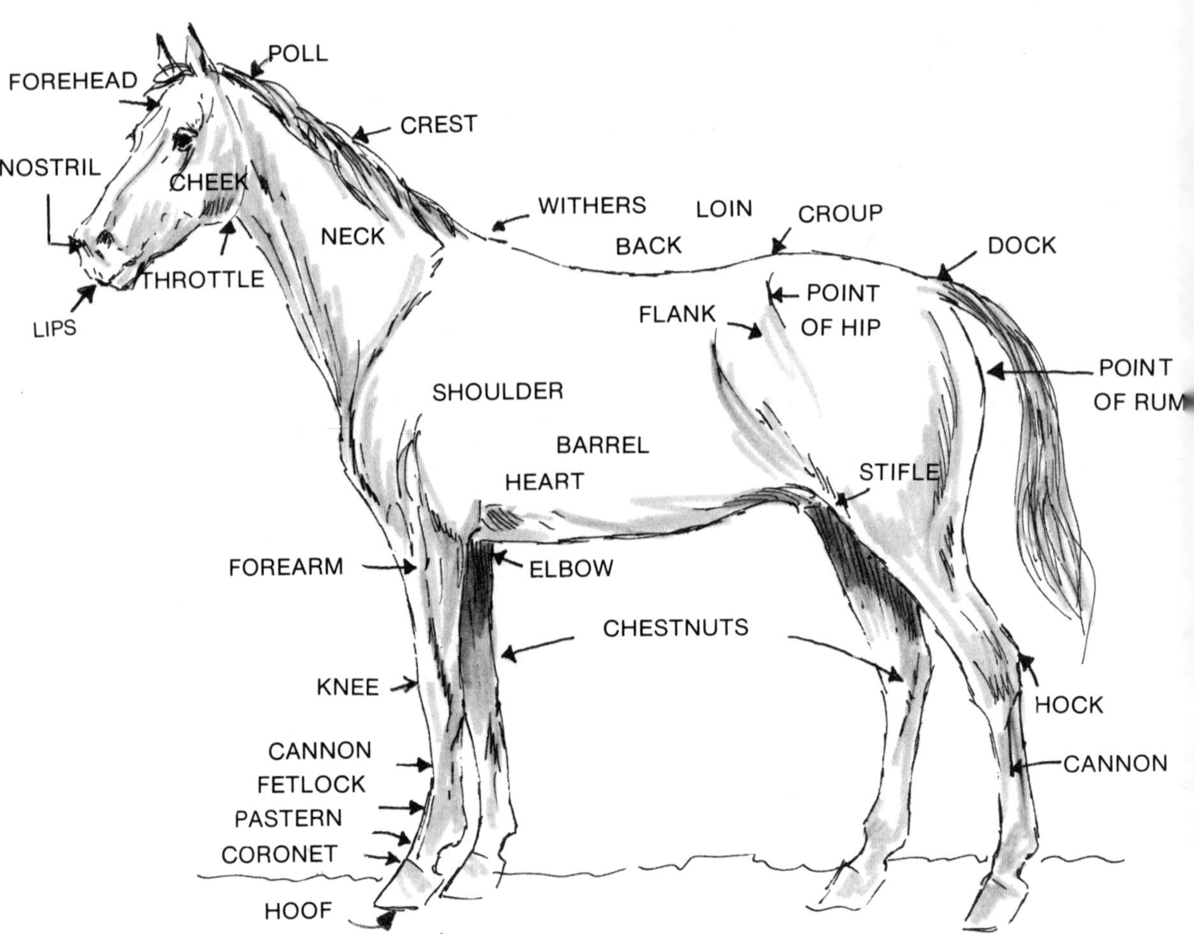

3 FINDING A PLACE TO RIDE

There are many good and proper places to learn to ride. The sources for finding fine riding clubs, stables, academies, and horse farms are available to everyone in the United States. The Yellow Pages of your telephone book are one source. Local newspapers are another. They usually list riding clubs, stables, and academies that are in your immediate neighborhood or close by. Local tack shops (stores that specialize in all kinds of riding equipment for horse, and usually rider, too) are another source. Family friends and relatives may know good places. The American Horse Show Association, Inc., 598 Madison Avenue, New York, 10022, will gladly supply a listing if you contact them.

The Place You Choose to Learn

The place you choose to take lessons is important. You and your parents should see the premises where you will learn to ride. Is the environment clean and the horses well cared for? Are the instructors neat, conscientious, and willing to discuss their qualifications for teaching?

Today's lessons cost an average of 10 to 20 dollars per hour. An average riding program consists of at least ten lessons. Lessons with qualified instructors are the only proper and safe way for beginners to learn.

Some riding academies specialize in trail riding where students ride in a group under some supervision. Other academies specialize in instruction at different levels, such as beginner, intermediate, and advanced. Your riding lessons can be scheduled one, two, or as many times per week as you desire.

Other places available for horseback riding, with or without instruction, are summer camps, dude ranches, vacation resorts, farms, and state parks. There are also bridle paths in city parks, paths down country roads, trails across meadows and fields. As you advance in your horseback riding prowess you may eventually want to display your skills at a horse show, ride cross country, go fox hunting, or play polo. Horseback riding will open a whole new world to you—you, the eager, skillful rider astride your well-mannered mount.

RIDING THE TRAIL.

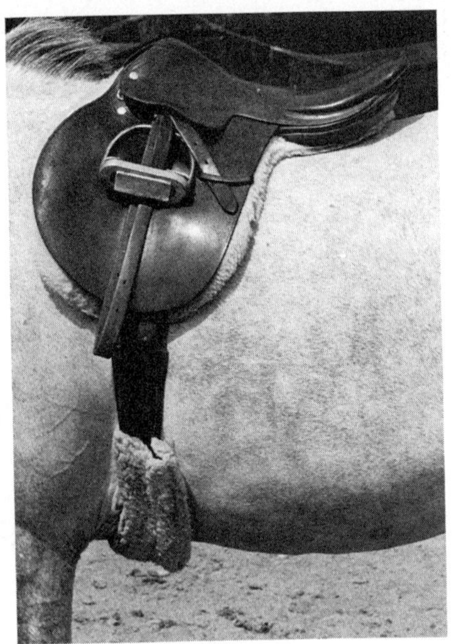

STIRRUPS UP.

STIRRUPS DOWN.

RIDER ON ENGLISH SADDLE.

TACK 4

The horse world has a special language of its own. Tack, in horseman's language, is the name given to any and all of the equipment that you put on your horse for the purpose of control, comfort, or training. Common items of tack are saddles, bridles, halters, blankets, pads, breast plates, hackamores, girths (called "cinches" in Western saddles), and martingales, to name but a few. We are only interested now in the saddles used in basic horseback riding.

The English Saddle

The English saddle is a light, compact, flat saddle. It brings the rider in close contact with the horse's movements. It is the saddle used for cross-country and trail riding. It is also the saddle preferred for jumping fences, hunting, and show riding skills. In the English saddle, the rider's weight is over the horse's withers, where the horse is best able to carry it. It requires more skill to maintain balance and coordination on an English saddle than on a Western.

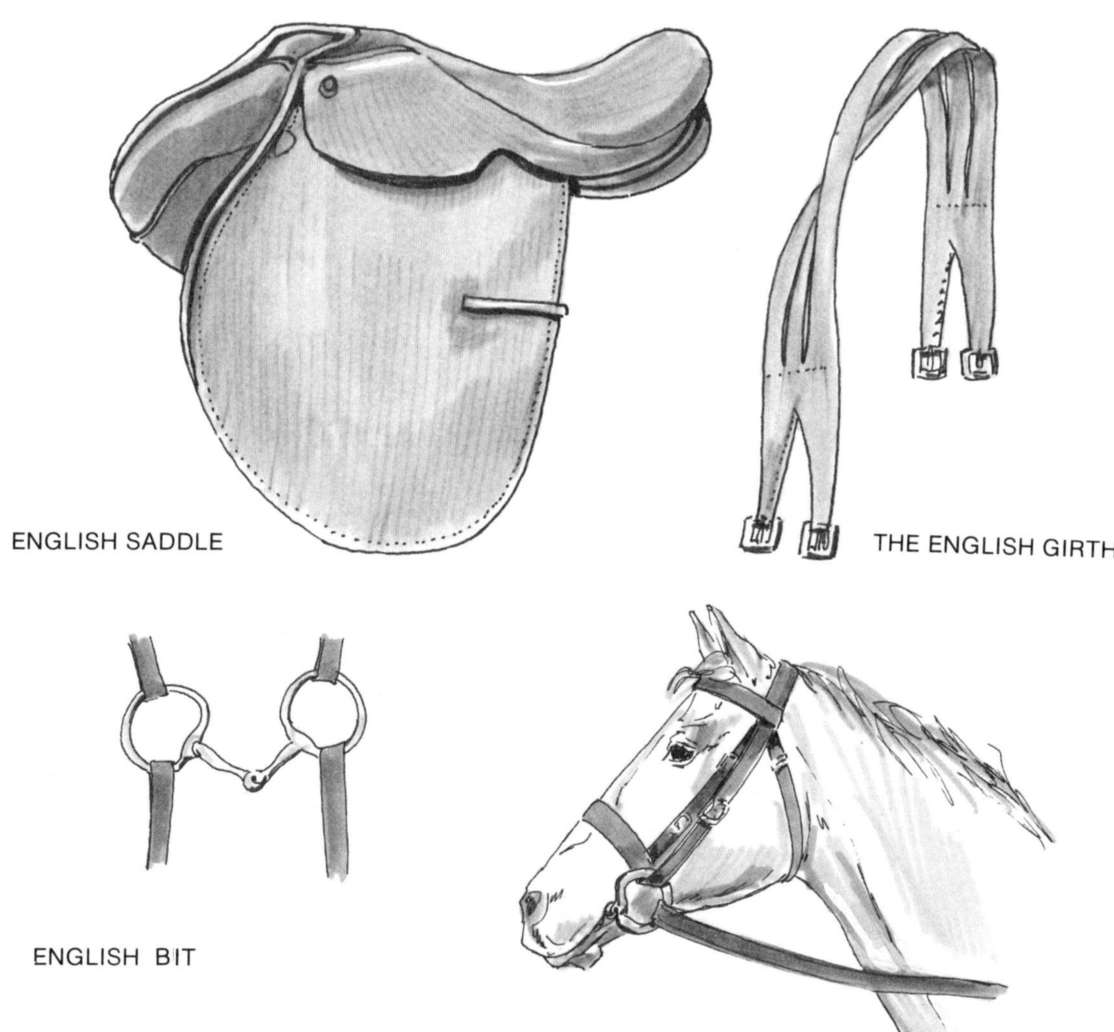

ENGLISH SADDLE

THE ENGLISH GIRTH.

ENGLISH BIT

THE ENGLISH BRIDLE.

The Western Saddle

The Western saddle is a stock saddle. It's a working saddle, heavier in weight and designed for rodeo and ranch work, as well as the show ring. It has a deep, comfortable seat and a high protruding knob, called a *horn,* at the front of the saddle. The Western saddle offers the rider great security.

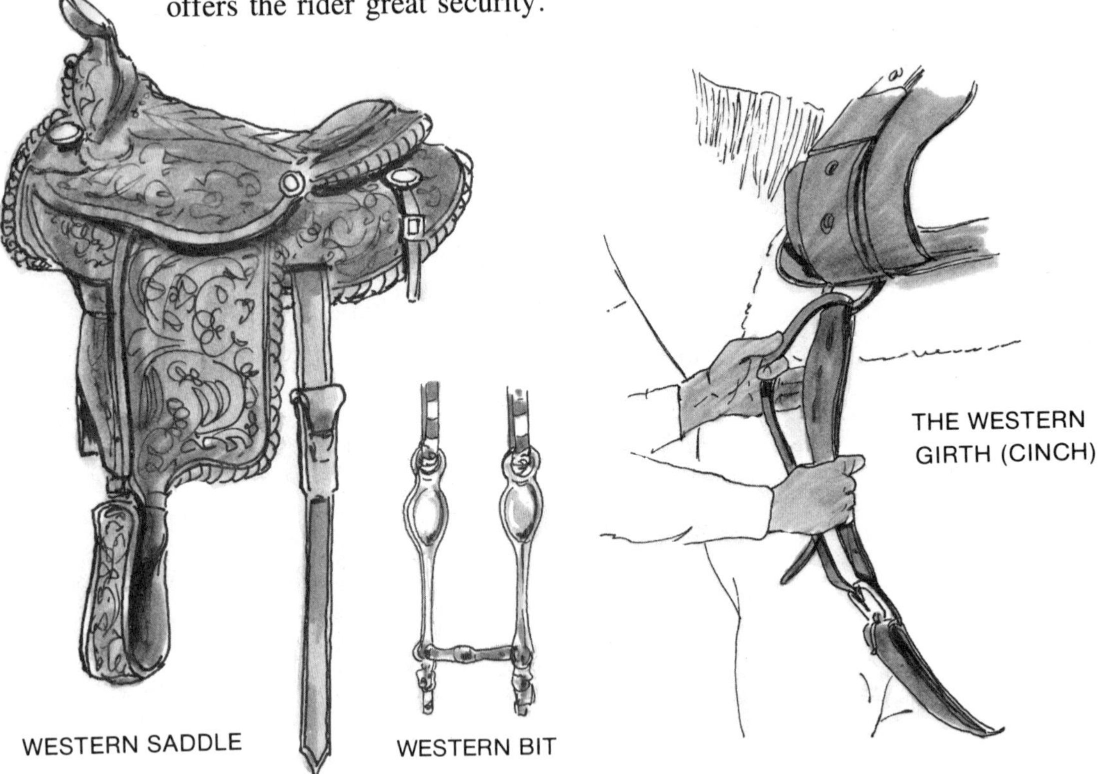

What to Wear

Horseback riding attire is flexible. It may be formal or informal depending upon where it is to be worn.

Informal riding clothes, for travel riding and for your first lessons, should be jeans worn with laced, hard shoes. A comfortable sport shirt or T-shirt would be fine. *Sneakers should never be worn.*

As your lessons progress, you will be more comfortable in riding attire. Jodphurs are pants designed for comfort in the saddle. They have a suede patch on the inside of the knee and lower leg for a tight fit and less chafing. Paddock boots are laced shoes that cover the ankles for better support.

A properly fitted hard hat or hunt cap is a must. You will need a riding crop. You can get both at your local saddlery or tack store.

At Snowcap Farm, I insist that all riders have their own hunt caps and riding crops for safety precautions.

For more formal occasions such as horse shows, fox hunts, and hunter paces, breeches (pronounced britches) are worn with formal riding jackets, fitted shirts, stock ties, and riding boots.

5 | MOUNTING AND DISMOUNTING

Preparing to Mount

Mounting a horse can be a gentle art, or it can be an awkward, clumsy performance. When done properly, it's graceful and effective. Approach your horse quietly opposite his left shoulder. In fact, all mounting, dismounting, and leading off a horse is done from the left side, or near side. Talk to your horse as you stroke him. Let him know what you are about to do.

MOUNTING IS DONE FROM THE LEFT SIDE. MOUNTING BLOCK MAKES THINGS EASIER FOR BEGINNERS.

Mounting

In the beginning, I believe all riders should use a mounting block simply because it is easier. Your horse will be ready for you to mount. Later, as you gain in experience, you will check your horse's saddle, bridle, and stirrups. If the stirrups are still run up on the leathers, you will pull them down and adjust the lengths yourself. Mount the horse by gathering both reins in your left hand. Place your left hand on the crest of the horse's neck for balance. Bend your left knee and put your left foot in the stirrups. Place your right hand in the middle of the saddle and with your right foot push up and swing your right leg over the saddle. Then settle into the center of the saddle.

You are now holding a rein that is too long in each hand. Without dropping either rein, move the right rein over to the left rein. Pull the excess rein through your left hand and then duplicate the pull to the right with your left hand. Always pull the excess rein from the top of your hand back towards your body.

To lengthen your reins, open your fingers and let part of the excess rein slide forward. (Your instructor will demonstrate how to lengthen and shorten your reins.)

To adjust your stirrups to the proper length, your feet should not be in the stirrups. The base of the stirrups should touch your ankle bone. After the stirrup leathers have been adjusted, place your feet in the stirrups. Now stand up in your stirrups, displacing all the weight of your body into your heels, and sit down.

Your shock absorbers are your hips, knees, and ankles. Your hips should be inclined forward, your knees should be bent, and your ankles flexed inward.

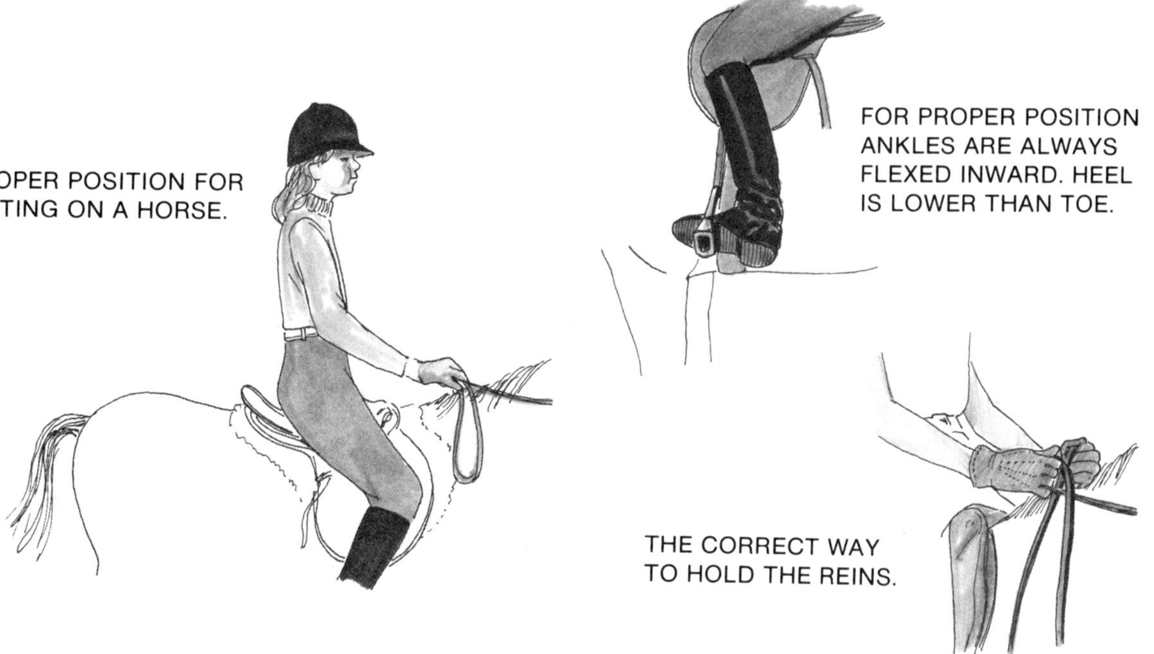

OPER POSITION FOR
TING ON A HORSE.

FOR PROPER POSITION ANKLES ARE ALWAYS FLEXED INWARD. HEEL IS LOWER THAN TOE.

THE CORRECT WAY TO HOLD THE REINS.

The Aids

The *Aids* are what help you communicate with your horse. They are the signals by which you "speak" to your mount. They tell him when to start, halt, back up, turn, and whether to go faster or slower or to retain his speed. The Aids are your hands upon the reins; your legs and heels upon his sides; your weight and position of your body in the saddle, and your voice.

Since any horse, even a small one, is stronger than a human being, you, the rider, must apply your aids to control your horse.

THE CORRECT POSITION.

Correct Position

Keep your head up with your eyes looking straight ahead as if looking at an imaginary or real rider. Sit in the center of the saddle on your pelvis, or "sitting bones." You will know you are sitting correctly when your crotch touches the pommel of the saddle.

You should always keep contact with your saddle, with the insides of your thighs, knees, and legs. Keep your chest high and your back straight but relaxed. Bend your elbows slightly and hold them a little ahead of your hips. Hold the reins tautly just in front of the horse's withers. Get your horse tugging on the bit but not pulling. The reins should make a straight line from your elbows to the horse's bit. Your legs should be placed just behind the girth. The stirrups should be on the balls of the feet, which are behind your toes. Your ankles should be flexed in; your heels should be lower than your toes in the stirrups.

Riding a horse may be likened to riding a bicycle. You do not look at the handlebars when on your bike; you do not look at your horse while riding but look straight ahead.

THE PROPER USE
OF THE CROP

Discipline and Control

Horses, like people, are different. They have different characteristics, different personalities, and different temperaments. Some are lively and eager to work; others are lazy and have to be prodded out of the stable. In either case they have to be disciplined. And learning how to discipline a horse is very important.

In order to communicate your wishes to your horse, you must use your Aids. Use them as firmly as you can and try to get the desired response from your horse.

There are other aids to help you discipline and control your horse, such as a crop (*quirt* if we are engaged in Western-style riding). Your instructor will demonstrate how to use it. To apply discipline with a crop, place both reins in your left hand. Now tap your horse gently, behind your leg on his flank. At the same time make a chirping sound, "Click, Click." Put a rein back in each hand again. This signal will help your horse go forward.

Whenever you feel discipline is needed, use your riding crop as described. Using a crop for impulsion (to go forward) instead of kicking is a much nicer form of discipline. Kicking your horse is not only unkind, but it moves your legs out of position and jostles your body.

Dismounting

Dismounting is relatively easy if it is done step by step and always to the left side. Of course, you will not have the convenience of a mounting block, and the ground seems a long way down. First, stop your horse. Your instructor will stop hers and will dismount. She will help you for the first few times, and then you will be able to dismount by yourself. Dismounting is easier than mounting.

Put both reins in your left hand. Take your right foot out of the stirrups. Since riders are inclined to ride with both feet placed deep in the stirrups, slide your left foot out of its stirrup so that only your toes rest on the stirrup iron. This is a precaution: Should anything go wrong during the dismount, you will still have a toe in the stirrup, and you won't get hung up.

Again, holding the reins in your left hand and grabbing a piece of the horse's mane or neck, slip your right foot out of the stirrup. Swing your right leg over the horse's rump. Be sure to clear it, for a brush or kick on the rump could be a false signal for the horse to move, or even leap ahead. Bring your right foot around to rest next to your left foot which is still in the stirrup. Support yourself in this position with one hand on the horse's neck and the other on the seat or cantle. Your ankles should almost be touching each other. The weight is now entirely shifted to your hands, which allows you to slip your left foot out of the stirrup. Now simply slide down, both feet touching the ground together. Bend your knees slightly as you drop down to absorb the mild shock of landing.

DISMOUNTING IS ALWAYS DONE FROM THE LEFT SIDE.

THE WALK.

6 THE NATURAL GAITS OF THE HORSE

In order to get the greatest amount of pleasure out of horseback riding, you must learn the horse's basic natural gaits and be able to perform them with safety, style, and skill. The best place to learn the gaits is in a riding ring where you can control and perfect your performance, rather than on an open trail where your horse may be tempted to run for the timber or dash back to the stable.

A horse can move his four legs in various combinations, depending upon how fast he is directed to travel.

The Walk

This is the primary gait of any horse. It is also the slowest, easiest, and most comfortable gait for the rider. In a walk, the horse moves one foot at a time—while one foot is in the air, three feet are on the ground. It is the most simple gait, and when done under proper bridle control, it becomes a smooth ride rather than a lazy shuffle. A horse walks at a speed of about four miles an hour. When a horse picks up speed at a walk, it becomes a slow trot, or jog.

THE SITTING TROT.

The Sit Trot

This trot may be posted, but it is usually ridden in the saddle. The forward thrust is not as strong as the full trot. By shifting your weight so that you are sitting almost upright, the gait can be ridden fairly comfortably. Sit deep in the saddle, bouncing as little as possible. The trick is to learn to relax comfortably while retaining the correct leg and body positions. The idea is to keep seat and saddle together. The Sit Trot is a good exercise for improving the seat and balance, especially if your feet are dropped out of the stirrups.

Learning to Post the Trot

The trot is the hardest gait to ride because the horse moves on diagonal legs. On the first beat, his left foreleg and his right hind leg move forward and hit the ground together. On the second beat, his right foreleg and his left hindleg hit the ground in another stride.

Only two of the horse's legs are on the ground at the same time. As he trots, the horse moves his legs alternately in diagonal pairs. His back also moves, bouncing the rider. Posting is simply rising and sinking back into the saddle in rhythm with your horse's stride.

At first you practice posting at the walk. Your instructor, riding alongside you, will assist. Shorten your inside rein and press your inside hand midway up the horse's neck on the crest. This will help your balance. When you have achieved balance, the hand comes off the neck in front of the withers. The reins are held in either hand. Ride with a forward and back motion. Rise to the count of one. Sit to the count of two.

Practice posting at the walk—stopping and starting again in a straight line until you feel balanced and confident.

Then ask the horse to trot. Practice rising and sitting without bouncing in rhythm with your horse's movements. Practice, practice, practice!

POSTING THE DIAGONALS (LEFT AND RIGHT).

Posting Trot and Diagonals

In the beginning, you, the rider, should move in a straight line. As your balance and rhythm improve, trot in circles and change direction.

At this point, posting will have become a natural motion for you. You should be ready for an exercise in diagonals. Trot a circle to the right and post in time with the horse's outside left leg. Then reverse direction and post with the horse's outside right leg. Your body should rise in your saddle when your horse's outside leg moves forward. You achieve better balance and coordination if you post on the correct diagonal when going in a circle. If you find you are on the wrong diagonal, simply sit out one stride and get into tempo with the correct diagonal.

THE CANTER.

The Canter

The canter is the horse's third natural gait. It is the most beautiful to watch and the most fun to ride. In the canter the horse springs forward from one foot and brings the other three feet down in rapid sequence. One back foot and one front foot touch the ground simultaneously. It is called a "three-beat" movement.

You can make your horse canter by urging him from either the sit trot or the walk. To canter to the left, turn the horse's head slightly to the right, activate your right leg, and thrust your left hip forward. To canter to the right, turn the horse's head slightly to the left, activating your left leg and thrust your right hip forward. Once the horse is cantering, relax. If you stiffen your lower back or push too much weight down into the stirrups, you will bounce in the saddle. The canter should be a safe, comfortable ride, like sitting in a rocking chair. The canter is a controlled gallop, which is what a horse does when he runs fast. Cowboys call the canter a "lope." In the canter the horse's head moves forward and back much more than at the walk and your hand should follow this movement. The speed is about ten miles an hour, although he can gallop much faster.

In the beginning you will probably bounce for the first few strides until you adjust to the new rhythm. But once you and your horse are together in a canter, it is one of the greatest thrills and pleasures of the sport.

TURNING TO THE LEFT.

Steering and Control

A horse's body will always follow his head. Keep his head straight and keep him "out on the rail" if you want him to go in a straight line.

In preparing for a turn with your horse, you must plan and "look into your turn." To go left you squeeze the left rein in your left hand and give it a slight tug while applying pressure with your right leg. To go right with your horse you squeeze the right rein in your right hand and apply pressure with your left leg.

For establishing control of your horse, pull-ups are the best method. Stopping and starting your horse while in his various gaits will reinforce your position and supple (relax) your horse. Your lower legs should be tightened. Develop a good seat. Control, balance, and confidence are thus achieved.

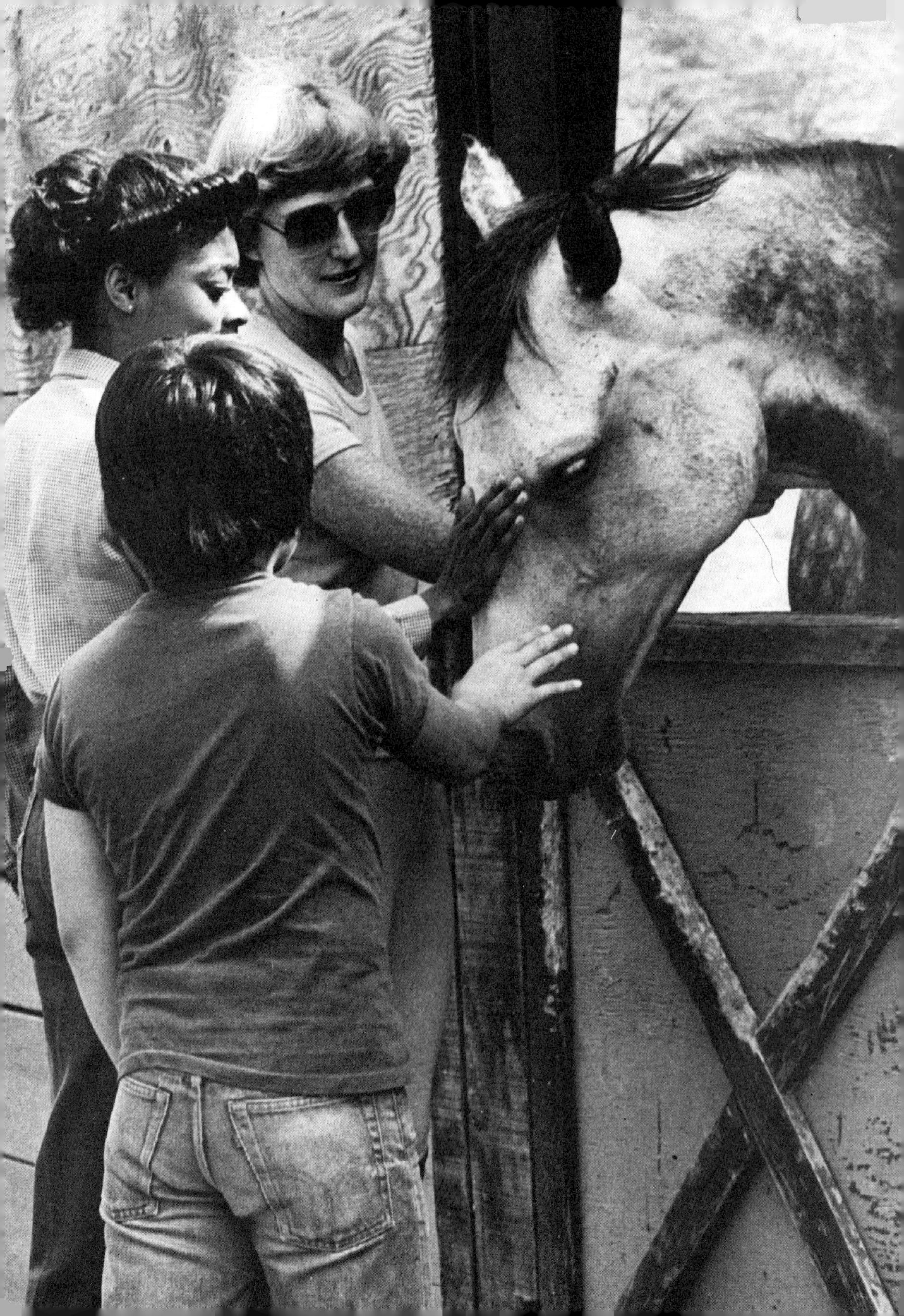

LEARNING HOW TO TOUCH THE HORSE.

7 | SAFETY PROCEDURES

Horseback riding, like most other sports, contains an element of risk. You must follow safety rules based on good, common sense.

A horse is a large animal with eyes on the sides of its head. Movements will be predictable as long as your horse can see you or sense where you are. The following are guidelines to commit to memory:

1. *Always pet a horse on its face or neck, not on its rump or flank.*
2. *Speak to your horse in a quiet voice. Horses do not like loud noises or yelling and screaming.*
3. *Never feed a horse without asking the owner's permission.*
4. *Never walk too closely behind a horse because you will startle him.*

GROOMING THE HORSE.

5. *Lead, mount, and dismount from the left side only.*
6. *When grooming a horse, start with the neck on the left side and brush back toward the rump. Then quietly move to the right side, start with the neck, and brush back toward the rump.*

When Mounted

You will often be riding with friends or other riders. You may be in a group or class situation or riding on a trail. Everyone must observe strict safety precautions at these times. This makes for greater enjoyment. An inconsiderate, unruly, or boisterous rider ruins everyone's fun. Always keep the following in mind:

1. *When riding, the distance between your horse and the next should be one horse's length.*
2. *Riders should never crowd neck to neck with other horses.*
3. *When passing, always let the rider in front of you know whether you intend to pass on the left or right side.*

MAINTAIN A SAFE, PROPER DISTANCE BETWEEN HORSES.

PULLING UP TO A STOP.

THE ARM SWING.

8 EXERCISES FOR SUPPLENESS AND CONTROL

There are a number of exercises, which a rider can do while mounted on a horse, to improve posture, suppleness, and control. These must be done in the presence of an instructor.

Arm Swing

Raise your right arm to the front. Swing it toward the back and around in a wide circle. Do this five times. Repeat it with the other arm.

THE TOE TOUCH.

Toe Touch

Touch your right toe with your left hand. Now touch your left toe with your right hand. Do this five times.

Neck Clasp

Lead forward and bring both hands together under your horse's neck.

Round and Round We Go

Cross one leg over in front of you. Turn in the saddle and cross the other leg over the horse's rump. You will now be seated in the saddle and facing your horse's tail. Cross one leg over the other again until you are back in position. Repeat with your other leg leading, going around the other way.

9 THE PATHS AHEAD

If you have developed a taste for horseback riding from reading these pages or from completing your first ten lessons at your local academy, you are about to participate in an activity that has no end. Your appetite for learning more and more will be ever active. But proceed at a pace that is right for you.

Much more technical information is available to you from riding clubs and academies that specialize in activities at horse shows.

Consult your school or public librarian for interesting books about riding, raising and owning horses, the history of horses, and showing horses.

You may enjoy the following publications:

The Chronicle of the Horse
P. O. Box 46
Middleburg, Va. 22117

Practical Horseman
67 Atlantic Avenue
Manasquan, N. J. 08736

They both list top-quality establishments throughout the United States and provide much practical information for riders.

The American Horse Show Association, Inc.
Madison Avenue
New York, N. Y. 10022

This association maintains a list of all academies, stables, and farms that are members. You can obtain information quickly with a phone call.

There is a special program called the Pegasus Program, which is designed to teach handicapped children to ride. For information write or call:

Pegasus Program
c/o Gordon Wright
211 Hillair Circle
White Plains, N. Y.

Owning your own pony or horse can advance your knowledge and skill. But there is much to learn before ownership. Let your instructor help you find a horse that is best suited to your ability at this time.

And, of course, write to me anytime if you want to know something more about riding and horses.

Dianne Reimer
Snowcap Farm
607 South Pascack Road
Spring Valley, N. Y. 10977

Happy and safe riding. I look forward to seeing you on the trail sometime.

GLOSSARY

AIDS—The means by which you communicate with your horse; your Aids: hands, legs, body, and voice.

BARS—The gaps on either side of the horse's lower jaw in which the bit rests.

BIT—The mouthpiece of the bridle.

BREASTPLATE—A part of the harness that runs across the horse's chest to keep the saddle from slipping.

BRIDLE—The leather head harness that supports the bit in the horses's mouth and, in combination with the reins, is used to guide the horse.

CANTER—A horse's three-beat natural gait, a slow gallop.

CANTLE—The hind part of the saddle, usually curved upward.

COLT—A male horse under four years of age.

FILLY—A female horse under four years of age.

GAIT—Any of the natural or acquired ways a horse moves.

GALLOP—A horse's fastest gait, a fast canter.

GELDING—A nuetered male horse.

GIRTH—The band that passes underneath the horse's body to hold the saddle in place.

HACKAMORE—A bridle with a loop capable of being tightened about the nose in place of a bit.

HAND—The way the height of a horse is measured. A hand is equal to four inches.

LEATHERS—The straps of a saddle, which support the stirrups.

MARE—A female horse over the age of four.

MARTINGALE—A piece of restraining leather worn by horses that toss their heads wildly.

PALOMINO—A horse characterized by his golden color and flaxen mane and tail.

PELHAM—A single-bar bit with a curb chain that fastens under the horse's jaw and to which are attached a second set of reins.

PINTO—A horse with a spotted or mottled coat.

POMMEL—The front part of a saddle that curves upward.

POSTING—The rising and sitting action of the body in the saddle as the horse trots.

REINS—Narrow leather straps attached to either side of the bit and held by the rider to control the horse.

SADDLE—The seat on the back of the horse for the rider.

SNAFFLE—A type of bit jointed in the middle with a large metal ring at each end. The reins are attached to the rings.

STALLION—A male horse over the age of four.

STANDARDBRED—A breed of trotting and pacing horses.

THOROUGHBRED—A breed of horse to which is used primarily for racing and showing.

TACK—Any type of equipment put on the horse or rider for the sake of comfort or control.

WALK—The slowest gait of the horse in four-beat time.

WITHERS—The highest part of the horse's back, at the base of the neck.

INDEX